THE OFFICIAL MANCHESTER UNITED Writing Book

LOUIS FIDGE

Letts

KICK-OFF

The Manchester United books are a fun way to learn and practise your English skills. Each book contains:
11 Big Matches, a flick-a-book player, find the cup, a poster and a board game!

The Big Matches

- Learn a new skill
- Practise the skill
- Flick the pages and make the player move

Play the match
- Test your skills (answers on 26–27)
- Colour in the Testometer to mark your score

See if you can find the cup hidden somewhere in each unit

Enjoy the pull-out game and poster in the middle of the book!

The Game

What you need and how to play

The Poster

Collect all the books in the series and the six individual posters make one big poster!

Contents

Verbs 4–5

Writing sentences 6–7

Captions and labels 8–9

Writing sensible sentences 10–11

Nouns 12–13

Handwriting patterns ..14–15

Adjectives 16–17

Capital letters in people's names 18–19

Writing questions 20–21

Opposites 22–23

Speech marks 24–25

Answers 26–27

3

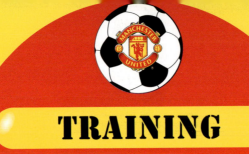

TRAINING

Verbs

A verb is a **doing** word.

The fans **cheer** when Manchester United **score** a goal.

Practise your skills

Write the correct verb under each picture.

cheering   scoring   heading   passing   tackling   throwing

1 _____   2 _____   3 _____

4 _____   5 _____   6 _____

Big Match 1

Choose the best verb to fill in each gap.

read   score   tie   comb   bang

1 You _____ a goal.

2 You _____ a drum.

3 You _____ a book.

4 You _____ your hair.

5 You _____ a knot.

flies   swims   gallops   hops   slides

6 A fish _____.

7 A frog _____.

8 A bird _____.

9 A snail _____.

10 A horse _____.

Colour in your score on the MUFC items!

Manchester United's nickname is the Red Devils.

TRAINING

Writing sentences

All sentences **begin** with a **capital letter**.

Football is a good sport.

Many sentences **end** with a **full stop**.

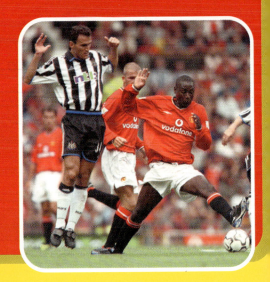

Practise your skills

Write each sentence correctly under the right picture.

| here is Andy Cole | this is Old Trafford |
| this is my favourite team | here are some fans |

1

2

3

4

6

Big Match 2

Fill in the missing capital letter at the beginning of each sentence and the missing full stop at the end of each sentence.

Colour in your score on the winning players!

1 ____he team won the cup__

2 ____y favourite team is Manchester United__

3 ____anchester United wear red shirts__

4 ____ome players come from overseas__

5 ____ld Trafford is where United play__

6 ____ootball is a great game__

7 ____ou can watch football on television__

8 ____very Saturday I go to a football match__

9 ____red the Red is funny__

10 ____eferees have whistles__

About 10,000 Manchester United pies are sold at every home game.

TRAINING

Captions and labels

In books and magazines most pictures have **labels** or **captions**.

Andy Cole celebrates a goal.

Practise your skills

Write the correct caption under each picture.

| Fred the Red | Some Manchester United supporters |
| Old Trafford | The Manchester United team |

1

2

_____

_____

3

4

_____

_____

8

Big Match 3

Write the correct label by each picture.

| shirt shorts socks scarf boot |

1  _____

2 _____

3  _____

4  _____

5  _____

| whistle studs flag goal shin pads |

6 _____

7 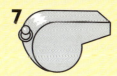 _____

8  _____

9 _____

10  _____

Colour in your score on the weights!

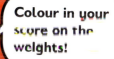

TRAINING

Writing sensible sentences

Every sentence must **make sense**.

The players is muddy. ✗   The players are muddy. ✓

Practise your skills

Correct the underlined word in each sentence.
Write each sentence correctly.

1 Paul Scholes <u>are</u> a good player.

   _____

2 There <u>is</u> eleven players in a team.

   _____

3 Some of the footballers <u>looks</u> tired.

   _____

4 They <u>was</u> not playing very well.

   _____

10

Big Match 4

Colour in your score on the coaches!

Choose the correct word to fill in each gap.

1. One player _____ hurt.   (was/were)

2. Lots of children _____ at the match.   (was/were)

3. The man _____ short hair.   (has/have)

4. All of the children _____ upset.   (seem/seems)

5. Every day I _____ to school.   (walk/walks)

6. Some lions _____.   (roar/roars)

7. A snake _____.   (hiss/hisses)

8. The ladies _____ singing.   (is/are)

9. Horses _____.   (gallop/gallops)

10. A panda _____ bamboo.   (eat/eats)

The first game ever played at Old Trafford was on 19 February 1910 when a crowd of 45,000 attended.

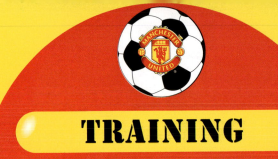

TRAINING

Nouns

A **noun** is a **naming** word.
A noun may be the name of a **person**, a **place** or a **thing**.

a footballer   a stadium   a goal

Practise your skills

Write the names of these nouns in the chart below.

person	place	thing
player		

Big Match 5

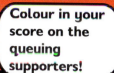
Colour in your score on the queuing supporters!

Choose the correct noun to complete the sentences.

clock   bird   football   ladder   bike

1 You kick a _____ .

2 A _____ tells the time.

3 You climb a _____ .

4 A _____ has two wheels.

5 A _____ has two wings.

car   window   shirt   school   boat

6 A footballer wears a _____ .

7 An adult drives a _____ .

8 A _____ floats on water.

9 Children are taught in a _____ .

10 You can see through a _____ .

13

TRAINING

Handwriting patterns

There are many **patterns** you can practise that help you **form letters better** and **write more neatly**.

Practise your skills

Trace over each pattern several times in different colours. Try to keep on the lines.

Good Luck!

- The aim of the game is to complete each part of the cup.
- You need a dice and six counters each.
- Play the game with a partner.
- Choose to be Cup A or Cup B.
- Take it in turns to throw the dice.
- Place a counter on the part of the cup shown by the number thrown.
- The first person to complete each section of the cup is the winner.

B

1. Manchester
2. United
3. will
4. always
5. be
6. winners.

Game

WIN THE CUP!

How t

A

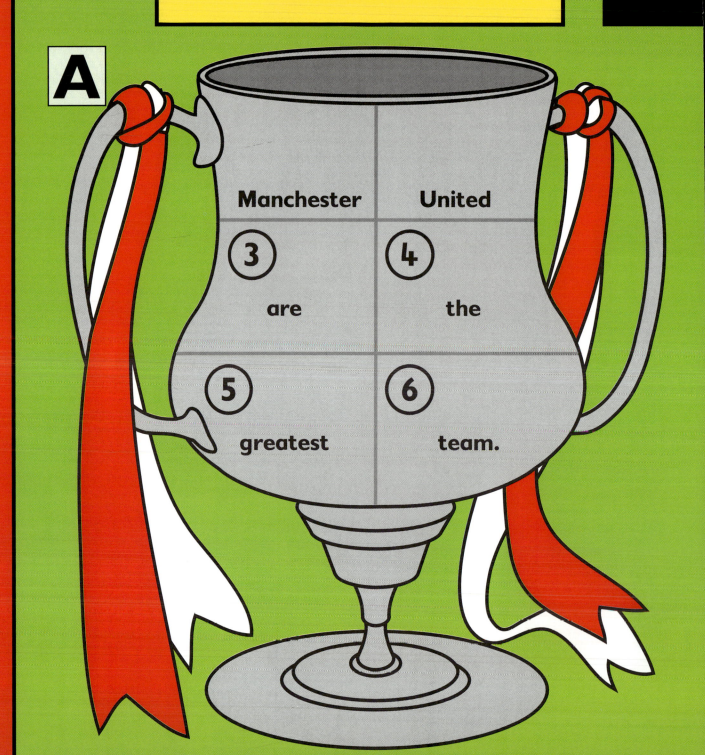

Manchester United
3 4
are the
5 6
greatest team.

Big Match 6

Trace over each pattern in pencil and do not take your pencil off the paper until you reach the end of each pattern. Stay on the lines!

Colour in your score on the exercising players!

1
2
3
4
5
6
7
8
9
10

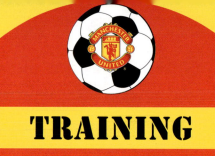

TRAINING

Adjectives

An adjective is a **describing** word.

Old Trafford is a **huge** stadium.

Practise your skills

Choose the best adjective to fill each gap.

black   red   white   loud   great   long

1 a _____ shirt

2 some _____ shorts

3 a pair of _____ socks

4 a _____ throw-in

5 a _____ shot

6 a _____ cheer

Big Match 7

Colour in your score on the kit!

Write the best adjective in each gap.

1. It was an _____ game.   (empty/exciting)

2. The pitch was very _____.   (muddy/orange)

3. Nicky Butt scored a _____ goal.   (low/great)

4. Alex Ferguson is a _____ manager. (good/dry)

5. The player made a _____ tackle.   (clean/cold)

6. The ball was _____ in the air.   (white/high)

7. The rain made the ground _____. (long/slippery)

8. Man. United are the _____ team. (best/worst)

9. The museum has many _____ photos. (green/old)

10. The Red Café sells _____ food.   (hot/wide)

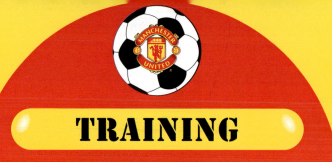

TRAINING

Capital letters in people's names

We always begin a **person's name** with a **capital** letter.

Alex Ferguson   Ronny Johnsen   Ryan Giggs

Practise your skills

Write the correct name for each picture.

| David Beckham | Paul Scholes | Jaap Stam |
| Fabien Barthez | Andy Cole | Dwight Yorke |

1 _____   2 _____

3 _____   4 _____

5 _____   6 _____

Big Match 8

Colour in your score on the cones and striker!

Write each player's name correctly.
Begin each name with a capital letter.

1 david beckham _____

2 roy keane _____

3 phil neville _____

4 ole gunnar solskjaer _____

5 nicky butt _____

6 ryan giggs _____

7 wes brown _____

8 henning berg _____

9 ronny johnsen _____

10 quinton fortune _____

On Monday mornings, as many as 800 pieces of Manchester United kit are washed at the club's laundry at Old Trafford.

TRAINING

Writing questions

We ask **questions** to **find things out**.
A question must **begin** with a **capital letter**.

Who are the best team in the world?

A question must **end** with a **question mark**.

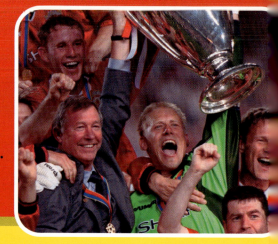

Practise your skills

Choose the best word to begin each sentence. Finish each sentence with a question mark. Write a sensible answer for each sentence.

Who   What   Where   When

1   Question: _____ colours do Man. Utd. play in ___
    Answer: _____

2   Question: _____ is your favourite player ___
    Answer: _____

3   Question: _____ did Man. Utd. last win the Premiership ___
    Answer: _____

4   Question: _____ do Man. Utd. play ___
    Answer: _____

Big Match 9

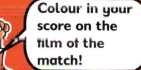

Begin each sentence with the correct capital letter. Choose either a full stop or question mark to end each sentence.

1 ____hat team is called the Red Devils____

2 ____y favourite team is Manchester United____

3 ____he defender made a good tackle____

4 ____ho plays in goal____

5 ____here does Jaap Stam come from____

6 ____ots of women play football____

7 ____ndy Cole is a striker____

8 ____hich country does David Beckham play for____

9 ____eferees make sure a game is played fairly____

10 ____hen were Manchester United formed____

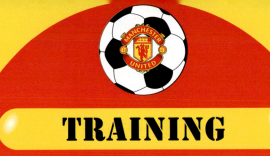

TRAINING

Opposites

Opposites are words whose meanings are **as different as possible** from each other.

empty

full

Practise your skills

Match up the pairs of opposites.

Write them here

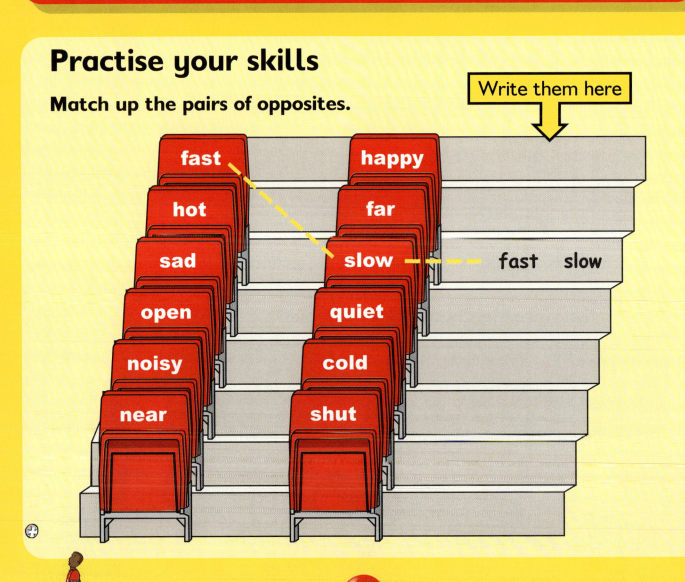

fast — slow

Big Match 10

Make each word mean the opposite by adding either **un** or **dis** to the beginning. Then write each word you make in full.

1 __un__ tie   _____untie_____

2 ____ appear   _____

3 ____ agree   _____

4 ____ pack   _____

5 ____ do   _____

6 ____ trust   _____

7 ____ fair   _____

8 ____ well   _____

9 ____ honest   _____

10 ____ lock   _____

Colour in your score on the shirts!

The Red Café has its very own red sauce specially made for it – and it has a picture of Phil Neville on the label!

TRAINING

Speech marks

We use **speech marks** to show when **someone is speaking**. Everything the person says goes **inside** the speech marks.

Fred the Red says, "Manchester United play at Old Trafford."

Practise your skills

Write what Fred says inside the speech marks.

1  Fred says, "_____
   _____"

2  Fred says, "_____
   _____"

3  Fred says, "_____
   _____"

Big Match 11

Colour in your score on the scarf!

Put in the missing speech marks in each sentence.

1 Fred says, __Fabien Barthez is our goalkeeper.__

2 Fred says, __I go to every game I can.__

3 __Andy Cole scores lots of goals,__ says Fred.

4 __Phil and Gary Neville are brothers,__ says Fred.

5 Fred says, __The players always train hard.__

6 __Roy Keane is a good player,__ says Fred.

7 Fred says, __I love Saturdays.__

8 __Dwight Yorke is a striker,__ says Fred.

9 __Footballers have to be fit,__ says Fred.

10 Fred says, __Manchester United have many good players.__

25

Answers

Verbs 4–5
Practise your skills
1 passing 2 throwing 3 tackling
4 heading 5 cheering 6 scoring

Big Match 1
1 score 2 bang 3 read 4 comb 5 tie
6 swims 7 hops 8 flies 9 slides
10 gallops

Writing sentences 6–7
Practise your skills
1 This is Old Trafford.
2 This is my favourite team.
3 Here is Andy Cole.
4 Here are some fans.

Big Match 2
1 The team won the cup.
2 My favourite team is Manchester United.
3 Manchester United wear red shirts.
4 Some players come from overseas.
5 Old Trafford is where United play.
6 Football is a great game.
7 You can watch football on television.
8 Every Saturday I go to a football match.
9 Fred the Red is funny.
10 Referees have whistles.

Captions and labels 8–9
Practise your skills
1 Old Trafford
2 Some Manchester United supporters
3 The Manchester United team
4 Fred the Red

Big Match 3
1 scarf 2 socks 3 shirt 4 boot
5 shorts 6 flag 7 whistle 8 goal
9 studs 10 shin pads

Writing sensible sentences 10–11
Practise your skills
1 is 2 are 3 look 4 were/are

Big Match 4
1 was 2 were 3 has 4 seem 5 walk
6 roar 7 hisses 8 are 9 gallop 10 eats

Nouns 12–13
Practise your skills
people: player, trainer, referee
place: stand, museum, changing room
thing: whistle, ball, boot

Big Match 5
1 football 2 clock 3 ladder 4 bike
5 bird 6 shirt 7 car 8 boat 9 school
10 window

Handwriting patterns 14–15
Practise your skills
(open)

Big Match 6
Scoring Score a mark for completing each pattern neatly and keeping on the lines.

Adjectives 16–17
Practise your skills
1 red 2 white 3 black 4 long 5 great
6 loud

Big Match 7
1 exciting 2 muddy 3 great 4 good
5 clean 6 high 7 slippery 8 best
9 old 10 hot

Answers

Capital letters in people's names 18–19
Practise your skills
1 Dwight Yorke 2 Andy Cole
3 David Beckham 4 Paul Scholes
5 Jaap Stam 6 Fabien Barthez

Big Match 8
1 David Beckham 2 Roy Keane
3 Phil Neville 4 Ole Gunnar Solskjaer
5 Nicky Butt 6 Ryan Giggs 7 Wes Brown
8 Henning Berg 9 Ronny Johnsen
10 Quinton Fortune

Writing questions 20–21
*NB Some answers may vary slightly.
Practise your skills
1 What colours do Man. Utd. play in?
   They play in red, white and black.
2 Who is your favourite player?
   (open)
3 When did Man. Utd. last win the Premiership?
   Manchester United last won the Premiership in 2001.
4 Where do Man. Utd. play?
   Manchester United play at Old Trafford.

Big Match 9
1 What team is called the Red Devils?
  or
  That team is called the Red Devils.
2 My favourite team is Manchester United.
3 The defender made a good tackle.
4 Who plays in goal?
5 Where does Jaap Stam come from?
6 Lots of women play football.
7 Andy Cole is a striker.
8 Which country does David Beckham play for?
9 Referees make sure a game is played fairly.
10 When were Manchester United formed?

Opposites 22–23
Practise your skills
fast – slow; hot – cold; sad – happy;
open – shut; noisy – quiet; near – far

Big Match 10
1 untie 2 disappear 3 disagree
4 unpack 5 undo 6 distrust 7 unfair
8 unwell 9 dishonest 10 unlock

Speech marks 24–25
Practise your skills
1 Fred says, "Manchester United are great."
2 Fred says, "I am a mascot."
3 Fred says, "My name is Fred."

Big Match 11
1 Fred says, "Fabien Barthez is our goalkeeper."
2 Fred says, "I go to every game I can."
3 "Andy Cole scores lots of goals," says Fred.
4 "Phil and Gary Neville are brothers," says Fred.
5 Fred says, "The players always train hard."
6 "Roy Keane is a good player," says Fred.
7 Fred says, "I love Saturdays."
8 "Dwight Yorke is a striker," says Fred.
9 "Footballers have to be fit," says Fred.
10 Fred says, "Manchester United have many good players."

Collect the set

Collect all 6 books and be an English and Maths champion.

Manchester United English

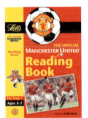 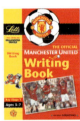 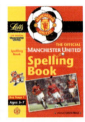

Louis Fidge

Manchester United Maths

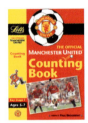  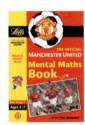

Paul Broadbent

For all the latest news, views and information on

MANCHESTER UNITED®

visit the official Manchester United website:

WWW.MANUTD.COM

Manchester United Plc, Sir Matt Busby Way, Old Trafford, Manchester M16 0RA

Letts Educational, The Chiswick Centre, 414 Chiswick High Road, London W4 5TF
Tel: 020 8996 3333   Fax: 020 8742 8390   E-mail: mail@lettsed.co.uk
Website: www.letts-education.com

Every effort has been made to trace copyright holders and obtain their permission for the use of copyright material. The authors and publishers will gladly receive information enabling them to rectify any error or omission in subsequent editions.

All facts are correct at time of going to press.

Published 2001

Text © Letts Educational Ltd. Published under license from Manchester United Football Club, Video Collection International Limited and Carlton Books Limited. All Trade Marks related to Manchester United Football Club are used with the permission of Manchester United Football Club, Video Collection International Limited and Carlton Books Limited.
Author: Louis Fidge
Editorial and Design: Moondisks Ltd, Cambridge
Illustrations: Joel Morris
Our thanks to Mark Wylie (MUFC museum curator) and John Peters (MUFC official photographer) for supplying material and their cooperation in the production of these books.

All rights reserved. No part of this publication may be reproduced, stored in a retrieval system, or transmitted, in any form or by any means, electronic, mechanical, photocopying, recording or otherwise, without the prior permission of Letts Educational.

British Library Cataloguing in Publication Data
A CIP record for this book is available from the British Library.

ISBN 1-85805-981-X

Printed in Italy.

Letts Educational Limited is a member of Granada Learning Limited, part of the Granada Media Group.

Supports the National Curriculum

Writing
Key Stage 1 (ages 5–7)

Now football makes learning fun!
With Manchester United, your child will want to learn and practise their English.

Make learning fun! Give your child:
- Flick-a-book player action for animated fun
- Pull-out poster of the players and themed board game
- The latest player photographs and fun cartoons
- Fred the Red gives exciting facts about the club
- Colour-in 'testometers' to motivate and record results
- 'Find the Cup' game adds extra fun
- Essential curriculum-based learning

Make your child an English champion!

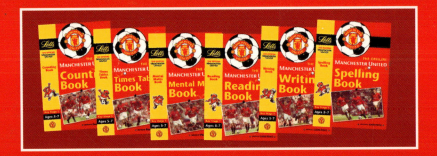

Collect all 6 books in the series and the 6 individual posters make 1 big panoramic poster.

www.letts-education.com
www.manutd.com

£2.99

ISBN 1-85805-981-X